Wings of a Butterfly
The Poetic Justice of a Domestic Abuse Survivor

Zanthia Boyd-Kesselly

"Perhaps God made butterflies to teach us lessons about life and make us more tolerant and less judgmental. We are all a work in progress and although were not butterflies yet, we can't become butterflies without first being caterpillars. We've got to eat a lot of leaves and do a lot of growing before we blossom into our final state. The caterpillar might not look like much now, but when God gets done with it, it will become a creature of splendor."

~ David J. Abbott M.D.

DEDICATION & SHOT OUTS

This book is dedicated to *GOD*, although it has been on my heart to publish some of my works for a long time...I now realize it was not in my time that it should have been done, but done in YOUR time. gI was in the caterpillar stage when I wrote most of this compilation. And today, thanks to your unconditional Love, Mercy & Grace, I have flourished into the Beautiful Butterfly that you intended me to be. With your guidance, I shall now be able to spread my wings and fly.

I would also like to dedicate this book to My Journey...To Life & Life's Lessons: The Good, The Bad and The Ugly! They made me who I am today. No Regrets!

To **Lionel "Micky" Beard**, had God not placed you in my life when he did, I don't where I would be today. It was you that taught me the true meaning of LOVE & that "true love" didn't hurt! Your love was the kind of love that gave me the strength to leave an abusive situation after staying for 10 years.
Your love was a love that I had never known before, you were and
will always be one of my best friends.
To this day, I consider you
"My Angel"

iv

To my mother
Frances Green, who is always my ride or die no
matter what! Thanks for always
being here for me...I love you
more than life itself.

To my daughter Tanae Irving,
my son Zyaire Alcerro, and granddaughter
Madison Irving Carp, all of to whom I will give
my last breath for. I love you with all of my
heart.

To my brothers, Richard "Ricky" Anderson RIP,
& Julian "Kevin" Anderson, who always
encourages me to be the best I can be & who
challenges my intellect on a regular. I love you
MAN! To my sisters Carolyn Jemison, Diane
Arthur, Etta Anderson & Richanda Stewart
To my best friend & Sister-Niece, Shannon
Jemison-Wright no one, no time or space can
ever come between us! We are inseparable!
"Family First" ~ 20204LIFE"!
To Stacy Stewart, Dana Turley, Enbrea Camper,
my GOD sisters OMG what can I say? Without
you all as my BFF's I am uncertain of how my
life would have turned out. I think you all know
me better than I know myself sometimes. I am
truly grateful that GOD made our paths cross
some 31 years ago and ever so grateful for our
friendship. I love you all more than words can

ever say. We will always be the "FAB FOUR" ~ even once we are the Golden Girls…

To Lawanda Gadson & Michelle Edmondson (RIP), my closest friends outside of the "FAB FOUR".. Lawanda thanks for all you have done to be a ride or die since meeting you nearly 15 years ago at NU…Thanks for all the long homework, business planning and book editing nights…luv ya 4 life!

Nora Taylor, who would have known that my car breaking down would lead me to find my buddy! You are truly an amazing woman. James Taylor, who was more of a father figure to me and a grandfather to my son than my biological dad ever was. I love you and miss you so very much. (RIP) Donna Taylor, my little sister, in God, I am so very proud of you for holding the Taylors down "Mama Donna"…

To Mr. James "Darryn" Taylor you are truly a God send into my life, through your story, I believe in the Miracles of God, God's Love, Grace and Mercy. I consider you one of my best friends and will always be your friend & ride or die solely because we are "like that"!

Here are the shot outs to those who have been in some way shape or form contributors to the "I" in me!

Forgive me if I miss someone..

My writing idol: Maya Angelou Whew, I am tearing up here, Maya your books have inspires me so very much. I knew I wanted to be a writer in the 4th grade after reading "I know why the caged bird

sings" & the poem "Caged Bird". I will always cherish your works. To my cousin, Grace Sandra Green-Ward you are one hellava' speaker and writer I am so proud of the woman you have become. Thanks for everything! To Lil Kev Anderson, Shanika Anderson Dezarae Dawson, ShanSharea "Rae-Rae" Dawson, Martez Wilson, , Bobby Croft, Michael Jemison , Mario "Red" Jemison, Walter "Pooh" Jemison, Sheldon Croft, Monique Croft I love each and every one of you "4Life" Any family I did not mention the list is so very long but the love I have for you is even longer! To my step fam: Linda Thomas-Boyd, Tracy Thomas, Delayna Thomas, Justin Thomas ~ luv ya to the moon and back! To my God Fam: The Terry's too many to name LOL Toshia, Meko, Nodi & Topaz Terry…You guys mean the world to me…
RIP: Walter E. Boyd, I love & miss you dad, Winston Allen, Greg "G" Gilliam, Kevin "Blue Gilliam", Kevin "KB" Beard, Elenora "Nora" Beard, Deante Beard, Damarius Simmons, Anita Ellington (I miss you so much Anita), Michelle Edmonson (I finally marked something off my things to do list), Demyus "Dbo" Allen, Mary Griffin, Lee Griffin, Tim "Sleptrock" Whitehead luv ya 4life fam, Kim Trice, Denise Taylor, Danette McClain, Holly Tatum, Devonia "Sapphire" Hudson, Sheila Smith, Yamora Williams, Jennifer Milton, Russell Neal, Jodi Neal, "K.O", Antonio Bolden, "The Nutty Boys" Corey "Pokey" Goss, Franky Rolland, Timmy Smith, Tony Kelly, Jay Johnson, Earl, Gilbert, Nikyia Suad, Salonica Rachal, Nina Wilson

Yolanda" Tangie"Porter, Lakeisha Poole, Kema Etheredge, Charlie "Charlie Lockwood (TY for everything! Brother in Christ 4life) Toussaint "Kip" Ware, Tanisia Baker (Author T.N Baker) thanks for all of the book writing advice, Lawanda Simmons, Larry Simmons, Camille Simmons, Charles Coats, Wendy Neff, Coach Curtis Simmons (Ty you for teaching my son all he knows about Football and being here for us ~ we love you) The Beard Family: I love all of you Charletta "Chuck" Beard ~ dats my dawg, Renee Gardner, Keisha Beard, Cynthia Mallett, Setitra Anderson, Julia Mallett, Johnnie Camper, Inez Stewart, Ethel Barkley, Immanuel Daniels, Latonya "Lala" Wise-Clark, Andre "Cazeno", Keisha Bullard and to All of my NU fam & grads "The Wood" Jeff Phillips my favorite English Instructor Ever ~ thank you for red marks, they made me strive for perfection! Delois Leapheart, words can't say how much I appreciate you during the after math of my abusive past. It was you who lead me to build a relationship with GOD & that I had to FORGIVE in order to move on! And lastly but not least: To my Family in Christ: First Baptist Church, Pastor Mike & Jan Stafford & Nation Ford Community Church Bishop Phillip Davis (RIP) & all of my brothers & sisters in Christ I love you...To all of my "I Grew up in Detroit" & " Detroit NC Connection" Facebook Fam where I can always go and feel at home! Not to mention get plenty of laughs. Lastly but not least, A special Thank You to LaKenya Cash for helping me pick a character name. Luv ya.

CONTENTS

1	HE BRUISED MY ME	13
2	ZOI A SHORT STORY	15
3	APETHETIC	23
4	SOUL TIES	25
5	THE PEN	27
6	SOMEONE LIKE YOU	28
7	BLOSSOM	30
8	ROLLERCOASTER	31
9	SMILING	33
10	THIS & THAT	34
11	PIPE SMOKE GREY A SHORT STORY	38
12	PIECES OF TEARS	49
13	REST IN PEACE	51
14	UNFAMILIAR PLACES	53

15 THE BLACKEST BLUE ~ EXCERPT   56

16 AFTER THOUGHTS   67

17 ABOUT DOMESTIC VIOLENCE   70

18 GETTING HELP   75

19 ABOUT THE AUTHOR   80

FOREWORD

*"I waited patiently for the Lord; and
He inclined unto me, and He heard my cry. He
brought me up also out of an horrible pit, out of the
miry clay and set my feet upon a rock and
established my goings" ~ Psalms 40 (NIV)*

I.
And then there were thorns...

He Bruised My "Me"

He bruised my "me", beyond repair…
The abusive effects became too much to bare.
His lies,
his fist,
his tender kiss
mentally drained me
til the "I" in me, could no longer exist.

He bruised my "me", beyond repair…
The love I once had became too much to bare.
His love,
his hate,
his horrible rage
emotionally impaired me
was trapped in a cage

So I wore this mask
In an effort to hide
the wrath of the pain
stored deep down inside
Swallowed my pride
To my pillow I cried,
While he continuously lied…
and made promises of change
That change never came
The longer I stayed
The more he stayed the same.

He bruised my "me", beyond repair...
Or so I thought
My "me" eventually was set free
the Battle was one
that only God could have fought...

Today he has been forgiven,
no longer do I hate
no longer a caged bird
but a beautiful butterfly
that only God could create...

ZOI
A SHORT STORY ~

You should have seen the way he beat up on that poor child. Ever since I can remember had some kind of hold on her. He had a lot of women so I suppose he had money, power and respect. To me he was simply a woman beater who deserved to get jumped on by all of them women that was claiming him as their man.

His name was Sharp and to me a real pain in the rear. He was tall and slender always nicely dressed, the clean cut type, you know. Ego was so high, Chile', anyone who tried to belittle him, specially, them women really got it. As I was saying, he had been beating that girl since high school.

Zoi was her name. Quite unusual name but it fitted her unusual personality quite well. She had many friends and I guess she must have had some sort of power herself, by having a man with power. She was kind of skinny, brown complexion and didn't get all that weight she possess now 'til she had that mans' baby. Gained 100 pounds and did them bones some good, I'd say.

That man still had beat that girl more often now, that he figured she didn't need to be hangin' out in them streets no more. I tell you one thing Zoi loved them streets. Ran into her at the bar one night she was drunk like she'd always be, trying deal with the stress that man done put her through. I suppose. I asked her, "Why don't you leave him?" Just cuz' now we was both sharing our stories of men. She said, that she had nowhere to turn. She slurred, "He Loves Me and takes care me."

Sharp could do no wrong by that girl. She loved that man to death I tell you. Don't dare ask me why. What I do know is that Zoi had this unique way of making his wrong doings acceptable. She would pick out some pretty cleaver excuses, in his honor, from time to time. I know by now, see, ever since that night at the bar Zoi and me got became real cool.

Zoi was really street smart and was the most intelligent "ghetto" girl I've ever met. And I've met quite a few in my days, Chile'. Most of em' either had street smarts or book smarts, but Zoi tended to possess both. She made a lot of sense most of the time, cept' when it came to that man.

Over the years, it has been about ten now, and things got worse for Zoi. Sharp had gone off and had four more babies, each one lookin' just like him Chile'. All of them babies had different mommas' too. Them women would always run to Zoi and tell her something Sharp had done for them, or to them, you know. Zoi would confront him with the things she done heard and Honey he'd give her a beating just cause, "curiosity killed the cat."

One day Zoi and me were sitting on her porch and this phone call comes from one of his children's mama; I forget which one now. Anyways, that woman must've said some things that broke the camel's back, cuz' Zoi wasn't the same from that point forward.

Never sleeping or eating and she started shedding that weight like she never had it. Zoi was on crutches; a car had hit her in 1982. This was the sixth or seventh surgery she had since then.

That poor girl was always going to school, learning something. She said, "If she didn't feed her brain, she didn't feel right." So she poured herself in to school. Started loving herself some, although she still stressed from time to time. I could see in her eyes, Zoi had pretty brown eyes. I'd swear people would say them eyes could win a million dollars, with the way they'd look at you. Them eyes would also give warning when she was about to swing on someone, out of anger, they say. You know the saying that "if eyes could talk", well let me tell you, Zoi's did. And they would tell it all, if you'd look in em' long enough.

Well, Zoi finally started seeing someone

else after all that time done passed. After all them years that man had dogged her out Zoi might've had 2 flings that I know of. And trust me I know. I think that even them two affairs was just her way of getting even.

As I was saying, Zoi was stressed out and lonely, she was starting to keep more and more to herself now. She was just as quiet all the time, talking all quiet and soft. If I didn't know any better I would have thought that killing somebody was on her mind. Zoi being quiet was unusual. The Zoi I've been knowing, that loves to talk and always got an opinion or always arguing a situation 'til she wins, her quiet now meant something was really bothering her. It was beginning to bother me too.

With all that mouth on her, she wanted to use it well off in Law School. That girl could write poems, raps and essays with ease. I guess you could say she had the gift for gab in any form.

Anyways, she met herself a man. He seemed nice at first. Let me tell you, I don't know what's worse emotional & mental abuse or physical abuse. I was happy for her though. He showed her out on the town, spent most of his time with her, and done things for her that, that dog man had never done. Put a smile on her face from here to China.

Them feelings started getting involved. But Zoi still all depressed cause she got this woman beater around so called living with her and all. To me he just seemed to drop by when he needed to change clothes or some good lovin'. She done been messing round with this new man for two months now, and he don't even know. Now ain't that some kind of relationship?

I guess one day Sharp started feeling some kinda way bout her, or just maybe he heard someone talking bout it in them streets. He really beat that girl bad this time. When she came my way no more tears Chile'! Just hatred peered through one brown eye, cuz' the other one was black.

That man had told her that she wasn't ever leavin' him or he would kill her. To be honest, I think he'd told her that many times before and she was simply scared to leave. Afraid of what he might do to her. Talkin' bout "The Blues". Chile, these was some dark "Blues." She did it though, she left that man.

Now, this new man really cared about Zoi for a day or two anyways. He came and got her from my house and they went off and got themselves one of them fancy hotels rooms, like they did three or four times a week. That man wanted to give Sharp a beating. But Sharp wasn't gonna fight no man. Zoi never wanted any trouble between them, she wanted Sharp to leave her alone and let her live her own life. Cuz' see, from the age of 17 Zoi had only seen life from his point of view.

Cazeno her Angel, as I like to call him, bought Zoi a lot of nice things. But she figured that he wasn't trying to have no kind of serious relationship, cuz' he was fresh out of prison and had some livin' of his own to do.

Could've fooled me by the way that man was hanging around, calling her all the time or coming to pick her up. This went on for about 4 or 5 months or so. I was sure that they were in love. Cuz' back two months ago that woman beater tried to run Zoi off the road and Cazeno got his chance to call Sharp out for a fight.

After that night Chile' Mr. Woman beater was gone. Oh yeah, he still called and begged and pleaded but it only seemed to make Zoi and Cazeno get closer. She really cared about Cazeno a lot too. Said she respected him cuz' he showed her that love didn't have to hurt. And that he cared about her and wanted her to be happy or at least she thought anyway.

Then one day out of the blue Cazeno stopped calling, coming around and Zoi was hurtin' all over again. Zoi couldn't figure out why. Seemed to me that either he had fallin' out 'of love as quick as he fell in or that he got scared off. Even might've been that he was simply trying to see if he could take her away from Mr. Woman beater. You know, playing some kind of game.

So here this girl is crying to me cause' she all caring a lot about this man. He done showed her so many nice times. Zoi told me that they never once argued. And that he never put his hands on her, in the wrong way and she respected him for that. Zoi said, "I will always care about him and he will always have a real special place in my heart." She told me, "that she cared about him more than any man she'd ever known in her life." I suppose, because he was there for her when no one else was. Cept' me! I was there from the beginning to the end. Zoi then whispered softly, "He kept me so strong." So strong that she went out and did something she needed to do for almost ten years, left Mr. Nobody.

Occasionally, Cazeno would come out of his shell and call Zoi. They'd spend some time together cuz' she had nobody else. A week or two later he'd be gone back into that shell again. Didn't seem to bother Zoi none cuz', she'd go on into her shell too.

That girl got tired of that too though. She gone on now. Moved away from all of that fast kind of livin'. Livin' life slow now. Working part-time and going to college. Livin'! Livin', for her and that beautiful daughter of hers.

Chile' sometimes trouble takes its course. Never changes though unless you put some effort in it. That girl Zoi, is steady shooting for that star in the sky. And in Zoi's eyes now I can see, sure nuff' can Chile', for once she is happy and content.

3
APETHETIC

Can't feel no more
Too numb 2 THE WORLD
Emotions are rare
Cept ~ for my own little girl...

Can't hear no more
Too deaf 2 the SCREAMS
Uncover my ears
Cept ~ can't hear anything...

Can't cry no more
Too drained of my TEARS
Wet faces are useless
Cept ~ they have fallen many years...

Can't sleep no more
Too tired 2 REST
Keep thinking too much
Cept ~ clarification is less...

Can't eat no more
Too many decisions 2 make
Overwhelmed with the STRUGGLE
Cept ~ the hungers' awake...

Can't love no more

Too much love brings PAIN
Emotions are numb
Cept ~ to love is the calm before rain…

Can't talk no more
Too many words went UNSAID
Swallowed with pride
Cept ~ subconsciously they were never dead…

Can't smile no more
Too bitter inside
Through clinched teeth, I HIDE
Cept ~ never has been one to confide…

Can't trust no more
Too many people are FAKE
Befriend you ~ then end you
Cept ~ so much is at stake…

Simply can't no more
Too tired and weak
The "I" in me can no longer find any peace
Cept ~ for that day when my soul is
RELEASED…

"The World hears Screams and cries Tears… It
can't find Rest from the Struggle and Pain, but
these things go Unsaid… So it Hides and
Wears a Mask… Until its soul has been
Released…"

S
O
U
L
TIES...

I sold my soul to the devil
for material things.
for benz's and jaguars
And shiny gold rings

I sold my soul to the devil
for all of the fame
Everyone in the hood
yeah they all knew my name

I sold my soul to the devil
for the money I made
and when it got hot
the devil threw shade

I sold my soul to the devil
became a dope dealers wife
for the abuse was so real
and it was my life

I sold my soul to the devil
for the love of a man
whose ways of showing love
was with the back of his hands

I sold my soul to the devil
Cash on delivery
Even though Grace and Mercy
had been given to me

I sold my soul to the devil
just like that
Jesus paid the price
So I just bought it right back…

The Pen

This pen of mine seems to guide my pointed
fingers in a conveyance of a latitude of
expressions...
~Sometimes I wonder~
Does its lavish ink conceal the literature within
my bold train of thought?
Or reveals...
It has a unique way of clearing up illusions for
my inner being...
Letting unwanted verbal passages remain
behind...
Freeing my existence for new meaning has
been given life...
Ink flows to paper so easily, controlling my
every thought quite ecstatically.
When it's tired ~ lays to rest
The Pen...
Yet, my thoughts always grasp hold
Of my dear friend again and
Again...

Part II.
Entertaining Angels

SOMEONE LIKE YOU
~ 4 MICKY BEARD ~

For all of the happiness,
my heart could
endure…
When not a single soul,
could have loved me
more…
To inspire my life ~
Like a blessing
riding on an angel's wing…
From abusive fist
~ to faith, ~ a rapture of finer things
So much joy and peace of mind
Never knew one day I'd find…

"Someone Like You"

In your arms it's warm
~ no fear, no pain
Just blissful memories
that will last a lifetime ~
To shadow an abusive past.

BLOSSOM

I find it hard to put my troubled past to rest
Somehow if I could ~ only past life's test
With you by my side how could I go wrong?
Your strength it helps to keep me so strong ~
you are my song.
A lifetime of me is all that I know
A lifetime of you is all that you show
As I sit in the past, in the center of rain
You welcome my love
and ease much of the pain
A grain of me found rooted in you
And with every drop of rain,
you encourage the bloom
So here I am ready,
to be the oxygen you breathe ~
Take care of my existence
because I truly believe
Without you in my life,
I'd be merely a seed.

ROLLER COASTER RIDE

Here we go on this crazy roller coaster again
Not sure if I can trust you
Not knowing who's my friend
Don't wanna love nobody but myself
Is what I tell myself?
No, not this time
Trapped in your love
keep wondering why?
I sigh when I see you
My heart begins to flutter
my words don't come out right
And my knees soften like butter
You send me mixed signals
I respond without thinking
Get all upset
there i go drinking
SINKING
Into my thoughts as
If they are reality
Envisioning us together
And your arms holding me
They say dreams never lie
Yet only a selected few come to life
The unconscious ones I hope for
Never seems to out sleep the night

31

You smile at me
I am not sure of the reason
Another season has yet to pass
I'm wondering why are you teasing - my heart
Although I am scared to love you
I care so much in side
An angel's on my shoulder
Whispering, "Sit Back & Enjoy the Ride."

SMILIN'

SMILIN' CHILE' I'M SMILIN'
SMILIN' CUZ I'M HAPPY
SEE THAT MA N HAS THIS MAGIC POTION-
DON'T QUITE KNOW HOW HE DOES IT
CEPT' I KNOW HE DOES IT SO WELL
COULD HOLD THAT MAN A LIFETIME
CEPT' FROM TIME TO TIME
HE BE HOLDIN' SOMEONE ELSE
SEE
SO I'LL JUST KEEP ON SMILIN'
AND KEEP MY FEELINGS ON THE SHELF…

THIS & THAT

WHEN I QUESTION WHAT YOU'RE MISSIN'...
YOU SAY THIS & THAT.

MAYBE THE STYLE OF MY WAYS OR SOFT
HANDS CARESSIN' YOUR BACK?

THAT TENDER KISS YOU'RE REMINISCING OF,
TENDS TO LINGER ON,
IS WHAT YOU MISS...?

THE WARMTH OF MY BODY,
I WONDER COULD IT BE THIS.

MAYBE MY SMILE INVITING ONLY YOU
TO LOVE ME LIKE YOU DO?

BETTER YET, MY UNDERSTANDING ABILITY,
THE FAITHFULNESS
THAT'S EVERLASTINGLY TRUE?

THE SWEET SCENT OF MY PERFUME
WHEN I'M MAKING LOVE TO YOU?

THIS SEXY LINGERIE
I WEAR TO GET YOU IN THE MOOD?

OR, THE LOOK IN MY EYES
LETTING YOU KNOW HOW MUCH I CARE?

WHAT? THE SEXY BEDROOM SECRETS
WE SO INTIMATELY SHARE?

MIGHT BE MISSIN' THE ORDINARY ME,
JUST CUZ I'M NOT AROUND?

OR THE SMILE I PUT ON YOUR FACE,
WHEN I SLOWLY GO DOWN?

WHATEVER IT IS YOU'RE MISSIN'
KNOW THAT IT WILL ALWAYS BE BACK...

CAUSE BABY IT COULD BE MISSIN' SOMETHING
TOO...
PROBABLY MISSIN' "THIS AND THAT"

Part III.
And then there was smoke

I have contemplated in my mind over and over again if I was going to include the part of my life about substance abuse & alcohol. Due to the guilt, shame & the embarrassment of it all, I've only admitted it to only a few! Therefore, I deleted "Pipe Smoke Grey" again, & again to later find myself content with publishing it after all. I will no longer hide behind the ugly truth of my past abusive situations including drugs. What is there to gain?

It no longer matters to me what the world thinks of me. I have been forgiven for all of my sins through the blood of Jesus Christ. The only person I aim to please is GOD, not man. Furthermore, "He who is without sin please cast the first stone"!

Although I started using drugs as a coping mechanism from the hurt and pain of the physical abusive relationship I was in for nearly 10 years ~ it's no excuse. I hold myself accountable for the choices that I have made, with no regrets. During that time in my life I was a caterpillar in preparation for the blessings & favor that was to come. The Will of God.

I am grateful that today, I am drug-free! And I sincerely want to apologize to all of my friends and family who I may have hurt or done wrong to during that time in my life. I am truly sorry & I love each and every one of you. (You know who you are) I ask that you find it in your heart to forgive me someday. **2 Corinthians 5:17** ~ Therefore, if anyone is in Christ, he is a new creation; the old has gone, the new has come ~ By telling my complete story to help others, I have earned my Wings..."The Wings of a Butterfly"…

37

Pipe Smoke Grey
A Short Story ~
Substance Abuse as a Coping Method

As I anticipated the next time that his abusive hands would choke me, or punch my body, I couldn't breathe.

My chest ached in fear, yet my heart loved a man that hurt me so bad. His voice could kill my spirit instantly, yet it could tell me he loved me while holding me tight. I won't sit here and lie and say that we didn't have good times. Because we definitely did. I exist lived for those times.

My abuser took care of me financially, after he forbid me to "hustle in the streets" to get my own. This is something I had done for a long time, before there was a "him". I had only obtained one job, in 10 years. Yet, I drove the best cars, wore the best clothes & shoes, and rocked the finest jewelry. With all of those material things I felt as if I "sold my soul" to the devil. And at some points in my life, I felt as though that devil was him, my abuser.

I loved him, I respected him, and I cared about him with every inch of my body. I would have done anything for him. But the thing I did most was I "fear" him.

For those reasons I could not leave. The

fear kept me there waiting, anticipating a change in him. Change never came, only another abusive episode. And afterwards, I was showered with apologies and promises he never kept along with "clear his conscious" presents. Roses, another ring, another car, or money for a shopping spree. Something to keep me around and in waiting for the next time...

During this time in my life although I had dozens of friends, and those wanting to hang with me and my social group. I felt so alone.

Many people question how a girl like me could turn to drugs. Especially when the mask that I accustomed to wearing showed everyone, my strength, my power and ability to demand respect... Little do they know, I was dying on the inside...Crying on the inside...Scared on the inside...Empty on the inside...Alone on the inside...

So here it is, Pipe Smoke Grey, the short story of how & why I started using drugs.

My phone rang, and a relative was on the line telling me that he was in the presence of "Easy E" of the rap group NWA, in Ohio. He went on to tell me that Bones, Thugs and Harmony was having a listening party for their 2nd album. He had told them about me and wanted them to hear me rap. I was so excited, after rapping for nearly 10 years of my life, this could be my big break!

There I was on the phone spitting raps like crazy for "Easy E". Priceless. Afterwards, he said he wanted to meet me and possibly sign me to their label.

I was so excited I called my very best guy friend and told him to pack we were going to Ohio. He told me that someone wanted me to bring some drugs to them before we left. During this time of my life I was a drug dealer. So I bagged some crack into a baggie, and placed it in my purse.

I then paged my abuser, boyfriend or whatever you want to call him and waited impatiently for him to return the page. I was happy to tell him what happened, but he never called back. So I left a note leaving the hotel room information in Ohio. Instead of him calling back, he came home instead because I was using the 911 code, when I beeped (paged) him. I was in the driveway placing a small suitcase and my purse in the car.

I followed him in and I very excited about possibly becoming a well-known rapper. This is something that I had wanting to do since the Curtis Blow days. Most of my life I had been rapping.

That night, along with everything else my abuser managed to steal away from me he stole my lifelong dream.

My dreams were all that I had left of me. After already being in this abusive relationship for 8 years, he had managed to control every aspect of my life. He was very jealous and controlled where I went, who I associated with, the cars I drove, or didn't. He even controlled the money to a certain extent, until I started stashing on him. I only started stashing because he had jumped on me many of times and had hidden the money that "we" had worked hard for just in order to prevent me from leaving him.

His facial expressions did not share my joy in the fact that I had just been on the phone with "Easy E" & members of "Thugs, Bone and Harmony" for nearly 30 minutes.

He looked at me coldly and said, "You're not going to Ohio to see no fucking Easy E or anybody else." I begged and pleaded and even wanted him to come with me but he refused. " I don't care if your nephew is there or not, I'm not going and you're sure in hell are not going to some hotel with no room full of niggas trying to fuck." He then yelled, "You might as well get that shit out of the car, and call them and tell them you are not coming."

I felt my heart drop. But I was determined to go, so I grabbed my jacket and headed for the stairs on the second floor of the house. Just as I touched the first step, he slapped me so hard I went tumbling down an entire flight of stairs. He began punching me in the face, then being choked until I nearly became unconscious. One of his friends was sitting on the couch and watched doing nothing until I suppose he thought he was gonna kill me if he did not let go of my throat. So finally, he intervened.

Blood covered my face and my already injured leg was aching so bad that I could barely get up. I don't recall how I managed to leave and make it to my car but I did and pulled off in my Black Toyota Celica.

I hit a few corners and then found a place to pull and attempt to clean myself up a bit. I had 2 black eyes a busted lip and huge scratch marks on my neck. My clothes were torn and stained in blood. My hands were shaking as I knew he was probably riding around looking for me.

As much as I still wanted to go to Ohio, I could not bring myself to go meet Easy E, with two black eyes, and ripped clothes on. I really did not know where to go that he would not come looking for me at. I didn't want to go to Detroit, where my family lived and was an hour away. I knew that if they saw what he had don't to me, they would retaliate with a quickness. Over the years my family had never seen the results of his abuse. I still don't know why I protected him in this way. I suppose despite of all of the beatings, cheatings and overnight meetings, as crazy as it sounds, I somehow still loved him.

Just then I remembered that I was supposed to drop off the drugs I had in my purse. The person who I was taking them to be a lady who lived in an apartment building that we once lived in. She was from Chicago, and although she got high on crack. She was a friend. I never understood why she choose to use crack, but I never judged her and gave her drugs from time to time.

Anyways, she had moved from the apartments to a duplex on the Westside of Lansing. So I figured I would go there and get myself together and figure out my next move. At the moment this was my only "safe place" or not so safe place after all. I remember when I pulled in the driveway I was very upset and still crying and shaking. My leg was hurting as I limped into her house. As I went in the door, she was yelling from the bathroom, "I'm back here." As I approached the dining room table I saw what appeared to be a burning cigarette in an ashtray and I grabbed it. Just as I was about to puff it she yelled "Girl don't hit that! It's a "primo" meaning that, it was a cigarette that had been mixed with crack. I was so upset, mad and angry, I said I don't give a fuck and hit it anyway. Before this day I had never did a line, smoked a "primo" or done any other drugs except weed, alcohol, and a few mescaline in my adolescent years.

After we finished smoking the "primo", it was like all the pain inside and out was gone! I can't explain it but I didn't think about anything except wanting to make another "primo". That high took me to a place where I didn't think about any of my problems at all. That night we smoked an "eight ball", crushed inside of cigarettes.

The feeling guilt and shame, I cleaned myself up and faced the music at home. Over the next few months, I thought about getting high, but didn't. I didn't tell a single soul that I had gotten high. Until, another beating came and another and another. I don't recall the details of those incidents, but, I do remember that after one of my abusers fits of rage, I needed an escape. Where could I go? Who could I turn to? I was so ashamed of what I was allowing this man to do to me time and time again that I couldn't bring myself to let anyone know the degree of my abusive relationship. Additionally, when someone puts guns to your head, and knives to your throat and tells you they will kill you if you ever leave them...You tend to fear them. I was scared to leave.

So smoking "primos", became my escape from the reality of my mentally emotionally and physically abuse life that I had grown so accustomed to. It became the "only" part of my life that my abuser did not control. Because he did not know about it. At first, that is.

I don't know how or why he questioned me if I was using drugs. But about a year later, he asked me. Although, I had begun using, I was only using it after the beatings and arguments to stop me from hurting and crying and being in fear. Which was maybe once every few months or so.

But I remember us laying in the bed one morning and he asked me. And as much as I enjoyed getting high and having "the great escape", I had never lied to him before and I told him the truth. I thought he would surely get angry and hit me, but to my surprise He cried, like a baby. He hugged me and held me and cried in my chest harder than I have ever seen a man cry in all of my life. To this day I am not sure if he realized that he drove me to using drugs, but I know on that day just maybe I had managed to hurt him just as much as he had hurt me over the years.

He made some calls, and within a few hours, I was in Brighton, Michigan, along with my abuser, my mother, his mother and his father, I was being admitted into a rehab.

There is so much more to this story, "my story", while I turned to using drugs as a coping method. Stay tuned for my upcoming full edition novel: *Pipe Smoke Grey*

It is not my intention to want to place the blame on someone else for the choices that I have made to use drugs. Nor am I avoiding accountability for my actions. However, I am merely sharing a part of "my story" in hopes that people will have a better understanding of what some victims may go through, as a means to escape reality when they feel they are afraid to leave. Using drugs and writing was "my way" of escaping the pain from being emotionally, mentally and physically abused.

Not all women choose the methods that I did, and may even find suicide as the only alternative. Although I contemplated that option more than once. My daughter was the sole reason I could not ever bring myself to pull the trigger. Many women who are victims of domestic violence, choice to cope with the pain inside in various ways. In some instances they choose to stay.

Although today, I do not use drugs, it has been a long road to remaining clean. The longest recovery period I have had is 9 years clean since then. I have learned to I live one day at a time.

I look to GOD in everything that I do and I have Faith that it is he who has kept me standing...Today, "GOD is my rock". And my relationship with Him is the most important relationship in my life, period! Without GOD, I would not exist.

IV.
Unconditional Pain

PIECES OF TEARS
4 MY BROTHER
Richard "Ricky" G. Anderson Jr.
May 30, 1961 – August 31, 2002
Burial: 9/11/02

i cried again last night,
the pain too stubborn to go away...
this constant need,
to speak the words you needed to hear
me say...

the future is, as i am told,
the destiny of God
but finding acceptance in that saying
~ Lately~
overwhelms me and is particularly
hard...

i try to find comfort ~ in telling myself
that you're okay...
no more hurt, worries or problems
to burden your life today...

no more struggle now
God is how...
~ your pain has been removed

49

no more troubled soul
nor heart that's cold
And still ~ i'm missing you...

things just aren't the same
seems like a piece of me is gone...
the piece
that in a time like this
would help to keep me strong...

the piece
that always made me smile
when i was down and blue...
the piece
that has me incomplete
the piece
that's gone with you...

i cried again today...
the same as yesterday
And tomorrow...
tears await ...
the piece
of destiny's fate...

Rest In Peace
4 Chad & Anita Ellington

Too many times I've wondered and still I do
not know ~
Why are those closest to us the hardest to let
go?
When I should be happy
That you will no longer
Struggle, Worry, Stress or,
Hurt
I try to think that way
But most times it doesn't work

When I think of your face
I want to shake you til' you awake
Knowing that I can't
I give my love for you to take

In your peaceful journey
Now that you REST in heaven
AT HOME
I want you to understand ~
that you will never be alone

Through us ~ the friends you left behind
Your name
and life
will always shine

In remembrance, you'll always be
Time after Time.
And

Now that you're gone ~
~ my world is Colder now
~ a missing Shoulder now
~ my load? a Boulder now
It just isn't fair at all
that you of all people ~
got the call
~ my strength slowly fades
~ and my backs' left to a wall

But

My ears still hear the songs we'd sing
And my eyes still see the smiles
that you'd bring
My heart still knows the love and the care
And my mind still knows
You are comfortable there
And I look to the Lord to walk with me ~
and hold my hand
Confusion still eludes my soul
Because ~ I still don't understand

R.I.P Anita… I miss you like crazy

UNFAMILIAR PLACES
"MY GHETTO"

Somewhere lost in the small, darkened corners of the universe hides many places; places that exist only for those who know of their existence.

Where life is meaningless to most and struggles are as natural as the hair of many men.

Where the streets are cold and lonely because every cause is for self, and flamboyance eludes from the loss of another.

Where crack babies cry out in empty rooms from hunger pains to a mother that is no longer there. Physically she exists, yet; mentally she is frozen to her surroundings cuz those surroundings to her are meaningless.

Where fathers are physically absent yet, mentally has acknowledgment of the pain their absence has caused in the lives of children who needs them desperately.

Where gunshots ring loudly and move quickly through crowds of many men.

Where police are less likely to respond in a substantial amount of time to make a difference. And at times they tend to let off their own frustrations from their own lives by means of a Billy-club or a 357 magnum.

Where many struggle to get out of the sticky situations or substances that they rely on daily, yet they remain stuck or better yet oppressed.

Where many brilliant individuals reside not knowing the capabilities they possess.

Where felonies keep those who have changed their lives, educated themselves and have tried to obtain employment but their past is smacked in their faces, by turned up noses from those who could care less if they provide for their families.

Yes, this place exist yet, it goes ignored, much too often.

You wonder where? There are many of them in every state, some worse than others, but most of those who live there are living there in poverty equally. This shadowed place you wonder where it is.

Shine those windows, place glasses on crooked noses and look through the door, there's a place that has existed at least 45 years of my life I'm sure.

Well let me tell you, "My Ghetto" has and will always be reality for me, yet nonexistent for others.

The buildings broken appliances, injured structures yell, from years of continuous abuse it has experienced lapsed time. The dirt that longs a seed or two in lieu of literal garbage.

Its' projects has many stories to tell if walls could only talk. The worn sidewalks' cries tears from the pain they know. more oppression would be in order.

How dare you should ever become, *The Rose that Grew from Concrete…*"(Tupac Shakur, 2009).

Excerpt from the Upcoming Novel

THE BLACKEST BLUE
By Zanthia Boyd-Kesselly

*Christians proceed with caution: This expert
Includes Explicit Language
& Strong Sexual Content*

Prologue

To this day all I can remember is being drug from the car by my hair; my back sliding across the graveled parking lot, and my already broken right leg being pulled by its' ankle. And the rods that protruded the outer right side of my thigh, being tugged at by the large rocks that shifted beneath me.

As I looked around the unfamiliar City Park, I remember thinking that today was the day; that he would come through on all of his sinful promises and deadly threats. As he held the 9mm handgun to the center of my head, my daughters' face, which was then seven years old, flashed before my eyes and my heart fell at the thought of leaving her to face this cruel world alone. I also thought why had I stayed with him for ten years? My mind raced rapidly, while I wondered what I had done to deserve this. What horrible sin had I committed that would make GOD show his wrath in such a way? The man I once loved, was now standing before me ready to pull the trigger and shatter my existence all over a parking lot, in a wooded area located in Eaton County. A county, that would disregard my death as drug related; or refuse to use taxpayer's money, to investigate because of my race.

My body was numb, almost as if I was apathetic. Yet, as I looked into his eyes for the first time I actually saw him for the, cold hearted, selfish, controlling, manipulating person that others saw so clearly long ago.

He took his left hand and grabbed me by the throat, and took his right hand and pressed the 9mm handgun harder into my forehead. I was scared but at the same time I was eager that my life would soon be over, and that I wouldn't have to suffer his mental and physical abuse anymore. "Who in the fuck is he Kream", he yelled. I recall that his eyes appeared lost, lost behind a face that I no longer recognized. His eyes looked like fire, filled with rage.

I could tell that he had been crying because his voice trembled as he went on. "I'm gonna ask you one last time, who have you been fucking?" "I know you been cheating on me, now who is it?" he screamed. Before he could finish the last word the gun hit my face and across the left side of my head. I felt the warmth of the blood fill into my eyes. I couldn't scream, I couldn't move and to be truthful I couldn't even hurt anymore.

I lay there motionless with my eyes closed praying that my life was over and that GOD would forgive me of my sins. I was too tired and too weak to fight anymore. I then thought how I loved my daughter so much and how much she loved me, in addition to how hurt she'd be if I never returned to her for hugs, kisses conversations and playtime, the things we both enjoyed so much. She was my only reason for wanting to live, my only reason for not giving up.

He yanked me up and leaned my body against a tree, his hands wiping away blood from my face, and saying, "look what you made me do to you." My legs felt like noodles, I was nauseated and I felt like I was gonna pass out. I'm not sure which of the blows he'd given to my face, head and body that hurt the most, but was sure that I would need a doctor if I survived. I needed stitches from the 9mm blow to the left side of my head that was now being given medical attention from my abuser.

It was true; I had "fucked" somebody else. It was true, I was trying to find happiness in another mans' arms and it was also true that during our ten years in the tainted relationship he had "fucked dozens of women, had six to eight kids, and had abused me both mentally and physically. Me, I had cheated on him 2 times and once was out of revenge. I had to ask myself, what is the definition of cheating? Was the definition wanting to be loved, respected and valued? After all I wasn't a possession or was I? Although it was true, in my defense I yelled, "Nobody Kaine". "I haven't "fucked" anybody." In an attempt to save my life, I calmly said, "Why do you think I am cheating on you baby, I love you, Storm." I then said, "If I wanted someone else do you think I would do everything you tell me to do just to make you happy?" I saw the tension in his eyebrows relax and knew that my words were what he needed to hear. I asked, "Why do you keep hurting me like this?" "Don't you love me?" "Is love supposed to hurt "Kane"?" "We've been together this long, I love you and I would never do anything to hurt you." I said.

The truth of the matter was there was a time when I would have done anything to make him happy, no ifs ands or buts about it. When reality hit me and I realized that he would never change, that he would remain the narcissist that he was, only wanting to control and abuse me, I needed out. I hadn't planned on cheating on "Kaine", it just so happened that GOD did is GOD thing and sent me an angel, and we fell in love with each other.

Kaine's eyes looked confused as though I was the abuser or as if I had hurt him as bad as the various bruises cuts and scratches that my body bore painfully. He walked me to the passenger side of the car and helped me inside. He looked me in my eyes with gun in hand and said, "If you ever try and leave me or let me catch you with another nigga; I will kill you." "Do you understand me", he said a little louder than his previous tone.

I don't know why but to this day other than my name, those are the only words I still can actually hear him say. When we began driving I noticed that he was fumbling with his zipper. This was not uncommon, that after abusing me physically he wanted to have sex, which made each blow he'd given to my body hurt ten times worse.

I fought back the tears with all of my might and tried to pretend that I hadn't noticed that he had pulled his penis out of his pants. He then reached over and pulled me to him and pushed my head down into his lap. Out of fear I didn't resist. I began sucking his penis slowly because my lips were swollen and the friction caused pain. Storm moaned with pleasure.

I must admit that over the years he had turned me out. Everything sexual I pretty much learned from him, he taught me what to do to keep him happy and I was eager to please him. I thank GOD that he wasn't into three-some's, orgies, or pimpin', because only GOD knows where I'd be today.

In any instance, me and his sex life was once adventurous and exciting. I truly loved him, and wanted to make him making him happy. But on this night I realized that the love was gone...That the sex was no longer as good as it once had been when I was lost in love with him.

Although, I pretended to be enjoying sucking his penis, bare assed naked; in the passenger seat of a car, while being finger fucked by him, as he drove seventy-five miles per hour at three o'clock in the morning, on I-96, I wanted to die. I had to fight back the humiliation and the pain internally & externally. I held back the tears and once again out of fear, swallowed my pride.

I kept asking myself, "How many times have you gave him head before? Or gotten freaky with him and loved every minute of it?" The answer was too many times to count. Therefore, I encouraged myself to go for the "Best Leading Lady" award, stuck the taste out of his mouth, and act like I was enjoying every minute of it, all in an attempt to save my life...

And the "Oscar" goes to?

He smacked my ass and said," who's pussy is this?" I fell into character, as usual and said, "It's your baby", while sensually biting my lower lip. Then he said, "You are my Bitch and I ain't never letting you go, you understand me Kream?" "Yes baby", I said.

He snatched my head back by my hair and looked me in my eyes and said, in a fatherly tone, "Yes what?" I answered, "I am your bitch and I won't ever give your pussy away or leave you, I promise."

I was mentally and physically drained, the only thing on my mind was doing whatever he wanted me to do, and saying whatever he needed to hear, in an effort to get back to civilization and save my life. I had saw deep into his eyes just how close he had come to putting slugs in my head. Although this was not the first time he had put guns to my head. In addition to putting knives to my throat, he had put a fear in my heart and taken my sanity.

I cringed at the thought of the numerous occasions he had choked me with his bare hands until I passed out. Reality sunk in that if I didn't leave him that night I would soon be dead. And there might not be another chance.

I felt like the dumbest woman in the world, to be blinded by his lies, control and manipulation. I was nothing more than a dope man's Bitch. Nothing more, nothing less. His narcissist ways had me thinking there was something wrong with me, and not him. I began hating myself for not being able to get things right, and for not being able to keep my man happy and satisfied. I actually believed I did something to deserve the abuse I was getting. Deep down inside I now felt stupid for going through this bullshit for so long.

Then all of a sudden, despite what all of my friends tried to tell me over the years, someone pulled the shades up, in a dark empty room and for the first time ~ I saw shit in bright vivid ass colors; and not as though time had frozen, and I was watching shit in Black and white.

By the time we entered the driveway of our home, my home, one of his many homes that now had become more often, his changing place, my body was exhausted. As I reached for my crutches, tears rolled down my face and preceded the mask, that I was so accustomed to wearing. I knew him better than I knew myself during those days. I knew he would want me to fix him something to eat, then he'd smoke a blunt while he watched T.V or he'd want me to beg him to fuck me.

My body was sore, my head ached and my self-esteem laid on the ground, in the parking lot where my brains almost laid beside it. I felt defeated. I was scared and confused, I had no fight in me left, and I had no life in me left.

Kaine had reduced me to nothing. I was nervous when I was around him. I feared that I would say the wrong thing, so I weighed everything I said on a triple beam before I said it. I didn't enjoying leaving my house because I was afraid he would show up and embarrass me like he had done so many times before.

Sometimes, I would be put on trial and asked dozens of questions about where I had been. I would be so nervous to answer them because with him twisting everything around and me stuttering out of nervousness, all of my answers ended up sounding like lies.

Therefore, I stayed home and sank deep within myself. I spoke to him less and less with each day that passed and I agreed with everything he said more and more.

I never feared that he would do anything to our daughter, because he was always gentle and loving when it came to her. But deep down I could tell she too was scared of him.

We had a lot of good times, he taught me lots of things and of course there were good days too, but I suppose that from my recollection the bad times out-weighed the good ones.

Kaine was a Balla'. He had money, power and respect. I was his Bitch and his punching bag. He was a walking time bomb ready to explode whenever someone rubbed his ego the wrong way. He was a hustla, but all of the money, jewelry, jags, Benz's, and minks had lost its value to me a long time ago, as did my pride and self-respect. Nothing mattered to me anymore except my daughter, she was and still is my "everything". I was apathetic, lonely and I prayed desperately needed an intervention. GOD was sending me an "Angel", I just hadn't realized it yet.

It had not always been like this for us. I keep asking myself what happened. Where did we go wrong? How did I let things go this far? Well to this day, I'm still in search of those answers. I was a young woman hustlin'- I when I met him and our story goes like this...

Coming Soon

By Zanthia Boyd-Kesselly

Kream's Blues

VOLUME I: THE BLACKEST BLUE

VOLUME II: THE GRASS AIN'T
                      ALWAYS GREEN

VOLUME III: SILVER & GOLD

VOLUME IV: PIPE SMOKE GREY ~
                      UNCUT

After Thoughts

To My Brothers: Love isn't love when it is forced or it results in the physical abuse towards a female. Forcing someone to stay with you out of Fear is the most cowardly way known to man to keep a woman. Ask yourself do want someone to stay with you because they want to or because they are scared of you? In 1 Corinthians 13:4-8, Love *is patient, love is kind. It does not envy, it does not boast, it is not proud. It does not dishonor others, it is not self-seeking, it is not easily angered, it keeps no record of wrongs. Love does not delight in evil but rejoices with the truth. It always protects, always trusts, always hopes, always perseveres. Love never fails. But where there are prophecies, they will cease; where there are tongues, they will be stilled; where there is knowledge, it will pass away.* If you feel you want or have to abuse a woman, pray about it, walk away, or get some help before you ruin her life and yours!

To My Sisters: You are beautiful with or without a man! You are God's creation, a unique butterfly in the making! You do not have to settle for less, just to say you have a man. It is never ok for a man to hit you. No matter how popular he is, how much money he has or how good he looks you deserve to be treated like a human being and nothing less. You were not created to be abused by anyone.

If a man does not respect you, you have to demand respect and sometimes that means walking away! If a man hits you once, he will hit you again. If a man can hurt you, he does not love you. You were not created to live your life in pain, despair or fear of a man or woman. *"There is no fear in love, but perfect love drives out fear" (1 John 4:18, NIV)*
And GOD has that perfect love.

Please respect yourself and do not tolerate abuse from a man, or partner, in any form. You are the creation of GOD and are worth more than you may know! Spread your wings and fly!

Most importantly you do not have the ability to LOVE anyone, if you do not love yourself. The best relationship that a person can have is the relationship that she builds with GOD! His love is Unconditional and he will never hurt you. If you don't know GOD personally, pray about God putting people in your life who can and will help you create an everlasting relationship with him. He heals all pain.

If are going through an abusive relationship please get help. If you even need to talk to me directly, my contact information is listed within the contents of this book. Do not hesitate. Your life is not a game, many women die each year, become permanently disabled and emotionally scarred from the effects of abuse.

Don't know where to start? Call 911, see the resource section in this book, or go to a local church, or hospital and they will help you. Again you can contact me, and I will do the best that I can to help you.

Psalm 10:17-O Lord, you hear the desire of the afflicted; you will strengthen their heart; you will incline your ear to do justice to the fatherless and the oppressed, so that man who is of the earth may strike terror no more.

Let us Pray…

"Father, I humbly come before You, giving You all that I am. I invite You to show me Your perfect love which casts out all fear. Fill me with Your peace and joy today and always in Jesus' name. Amen" (Olsteen, 2015).

About Physical & Domestic Abuse

Physical abuse is violence that causes a person pain, an impairment of any kind, or bodily harm. Physical abuse may include a variety of things including assaulting, restraining, hitting, kicking, punching, slapping or even shoving another person.

Domestic violence is when physical abuse occurs between the victim and a spouse or intimate partner. According to the National Coalition against Domestic Violence (NCADV), domestic violence is the willful intimidation, physical assault, battery, sexual assault, and/or other abusive behavior as part of a systematic pattern of power and control perpetrated by one intimate partner against another. It includes physical violence, sexual violence, psychological violence, and emotional abuse.

It is reported that "every 9 seconds in the US, a woman is assaulted or beaten" and "On average, nearly 20 people per minute are physically abused by an intimate partner in the United States" (NCADV).

THE SIGNS OF ABUSE

It might not be easy to identify domestic violence at first. While some relationships are clearly abusive from the outset, abuse often starts subtly and gets worse over time." (Mayo Clinic, 2014) Symptoms are both internal and external within the perimeters of the relationship. Signs can be physical, emotional and even behavioral. Obvious signs are things we can see with the eye. A cut, bruise, scratches etc. Even though these signs are apparent, many women will try and cover them up and hide them.

In most instances the signs appear in the woman's emotional stability, long after the bruises are gone. A woman will tend to feel as though she is the cause for the abusers violent actions. At this point the victim tends to shy away from her normal social activities (due to depression) and even begin to walk on "egg shells" and become nervous and tense out of fear.

When physical abuse is inflicted on a woman by a spouse or intimate partner it is typically due the abuser attempting to gain power and control of the victim by force, intimidation and fear. At times an abuser will use various tactics to manipulate a women and use their power: Dominance, Humiliation, Isolation, Threats, Intimidation, Denial & Blame (Helping Guide).

- When an abuser uses *dominance*, they feel the need to be in charge of every aspect of the relationship. They will control where a woman goes, what she does, what she wears, and how she behaves herself, and even how and when to spend money. In most cases a woman is treated more like a child instead of an adult.
- An abuser will use *humiliation*, they typically try to do things to make the woman feel bad about herself.
- An abuser uses *isolation* it is primary done so to make the woman become dependent solely on him.
- *Intimidation* is used by abusers as a scare tactic. This tactic typically means that if a woman does not submit to his demands, there will be consequences such as physical abuse.

Physical abuse has both short term and long term effects. The effects of physical abuse can be intense. A woman may experience immediate effects of physical abuse, as the result of being hit. The short term effects of physical abuse and domestic violence are: "bruises, broken bones, head injuries, lacerations, and internal bleeding" (Shahzadi, et al., 2012).

Long-term effects are more severe, and the woman nay suffer from post-traumatic stress disorder. In some cases the effects are more profound and could even end in the death of the victim. An important factor to note when mentioning the effects of physical abuse, is that it is not always the victim who suffers. In many instances the victims children suffer from the effects of abuse as well. Additional long-term effects include: depression, anxiety, low self-esteem. "The more severe the abuse, the greater its impact on a woman's physical and mental health" (Clinton & Langberg, 2011).

Additionally, women who are in or have been in a domestically violent relationship, tends to turn to drugs and alcohol as coping methods. "According to research, abused women have a 16-times greater risk of abusing alcohol and a 9-times greater risk of abusing drugs when compared to non-abused women" (Helping Guide).

Getting Help

The primary concern when dealing with someone who is a victim or has been a victim of domestic violence is safety. "Working out a safety plan for the victim is essential". (Clinton, 2011). According to Safe Horizon, for some survivors of domestic violence, it is developing a plan ahead of time is helpful to have in the event of another violent episode or when they feel emotionally overwhelmed.

If someone is in a current violent situation it is important to advise the victim of ways and places she can get help.

Many times when women leave their abusers, they forced to leave their homes, jobs and the majority of their personal belongings. Therefore, being able to located and provide various community resources to help the victim "pick up the pieces" will be important.

DOMESTIC VIOLENCE
HELP & SUPPORT

According to research, 1 in 4 women will experience domestic violence during her lifetime. And 1 in 3 female homicide victims are murdered by their current or former partner every year. (Safehorizon).

If you are a victim of domestic violence or you know someone who is please get help now. There are places that will provide safe housing for victims, legal advocacy and counseling for them and their children free of charge.

Leaving is sometimes the hardest thing to do. But leaving may be the only way to save your life. Remember we can never change someone else, but we always change ourselves. The following numbers can help you "change thangz".

THE NATIONAL DOMESTIC VIOLENCE HOTLINE: The Hotline provides lifesaving tools and immediate support to enable victims to find safety and live lives free of abuse. Resources and help can be found by calling 1-800-799-SAFE (7233) or for Deaf callers on video phone 1-855-812-1001 (Monday to Friday, 9 a.m. – 5 p.m. PST) or TTY 1-800-787-3224. www.thehotline.org

NATIONAL SEXUAL ASSAULT HOTLINE
1-800-656-HOPE (4673)
NATIONAL TEEN DATING ABUSE HELPLINE
1-866-331-9474 1-866-331-8453 (TTY)

Resources in Michigan:
Detroit
Wayne County
YWCA/Interim House Metro Detroit
Address: P.O. Box 21904
Detroit, MI 48221
Phone: (313) 862-3580 Fax: (313) 862-4190
Crisis: (313) 862-5300
Website:
www.ywcadetroit.org/our_programs/domesti

c_violence_services/interim_house.html

Wayne County SAFE Program
Address: Detroit, MI 48234
Phone: (313) 964-9701
Fax: (313) 369-5501
Crisis: (313) 430-8000

First Step
Address: Plymouth, MI 48170-3840
Phone: (734) 416-1111
Fax: (734) 416-5555
Crisis: (734) 459-5900 or 1-888-453-5900

Lansing
Ingham & Eaton Counties

EVE, Inc.
Address:
P.O. Box 14149
Lansing, MI 48901
Phone: (517) 372-5976
Fax: (517) 702-9908
Crisis: (517) 372-5572
Web Site: http://www.eveinc.org

SIREN / Eaton Shelter
Address:
P.O. Box 369
245 S. Cochran Ave.
Charlotte, MI 48813
Phone: (517) 543-0748
Fax: (517) 543-0883
Crisis: (517) 543-4915 or 1-800-899-9997
Website:
  http://www.sireneatonshelter.org/

Resources in North Carolina

Charlotte
Mecklenburg County

Safe Alliance - The Shelter for Battered Women
601 East Fifth Street, Suite 400
Charlotte, NC 28202
Office: (704) 332-9034
Crisis: (704) 332-2513
Fax: (704) 373.1604
Website: www.safealliance.org

Safe Alliance - Victim Assistance
720 East 4th Street, Room 204
Charlotte, NC 28202
Office: (704) 336-4126
Crisis: Shelter for Battered Women
(704) 332-2513
Fax: (704) 336-4416

Mecklenburg County Women's Commission
700 North Tryon St.
Hal Marshall Building
Charlotte, NC 28202
Office: (704) 336-3210
Fax: (704) 336-4198
Website: css.charmeck.org

Resources in South Carolina
Rock Hill
York County

Safe Passage Inc.
Domestic Violence Services – York, Chester, and Lancaster
Sexual Assault Services – York and Union
Phone: 803-329-3336 Hotline: 1-800-659-0977
www.safepassagesc.org

ABOUT THE AUTHOR

ZANTHIA BOYD-KESSELLY

Zanthia Boyd was born and raised in Detroit, Michigan. She grew up in a domestically abusive household until her parents divorced when she was nine. Her mother moved the family to Lansing, Michigan at the age of fourteen years old. It was then that she befriended Stacy Stewart, Dana Turley & Enbrea Camper who after thirty-one years are still best friends.

Zanthia is the mother of two children: Tanae Irving, twenty-five years old & Zyaire Alcerro, whom is seven years old . She is proud grandmother of 3 year old Madison Irving-Carp.

Zanthia was in an abusive relationship from sixteen years old until she was twenty-six years old. When she left her abuser she moved away and attended Northwood University. It was then she built an everlasting relationship with God.

After obtaining her Bachelor's Degree, she worked for several Fortune 500 companies including: Dow Chemical Company & Michigan Bell Company. In 2005, she moved to Charlotte, NC where she resided with her family for 9 years.

As a Christian single mother Zanthia currently resides in South Carolina. She has volunteered with Charlotte's Speakers Bureau, P.E.A.R.L.S and various Domestic Violence Organizations over the years.

She has facilitated Bible Studies at her church, and has been an Alter greeter for those who commit their lives to Christ.

Zanthia currently volunteers at a Christian Women's Job Corps assisting women who have had challenges in life including but not limited to domestic violence.

Currently, Zanthia is working on her Master's Degree at Liberty University to obtain a degree in Human Services Counseling: Marriage and Family and would like to start her own non-profit to help women of all walks of life.

She is packed full of resources and has the heart to want to save the world and will help anyone in need. She has been a huge help to her community with her acts of kindness and eagerness to help out anyone she meets. She has "never met a stranger". Some consider her a "Jack of All Trades" and a walking "Wikipedia" and has been known as "Zikipedia". After being through so many trials and tribulations by God's Grace & Mercy she is "Still Standing" for I truly believe she is a "Phenomenal Woman".

"Perfect Love" By Joel Osteen

" God is love. He is perfect, and His love for us is perfect. There is nothing you can do right now to make God love you more, and there's nothing you can do to make Him love you any less. His love toward you is steadfast; it's unchanging. His arms are always stretched out toward you. He's always ready for you to come to Him.

Sometimes people aren't sure how God feels about them. They think He might be mad at them, but Scripture tells us just the opposite. God's not mad at you; He's madly in love with you! It doesn't matter what you've done or where you've come from, God's arms are open to you. He's longing to show you His goodness and grace.

Today, meditate on the truth that it is His kindness that leads us to repent and change our ways. Open your heart and receive His love. Let it give you confidence and make you new. Trust His perfect love and let Him transform every area of your life"
(Joel Olsteen, 2015.)

Booking Request & Victim Contact Request

Domestic Violence & Substance Abuse
Speaking Engagements
And
Those who may needs words of
encouragement, guidance, empowerment
referrals to get help.
If your situation is an emergency
please call 911
Otherwise
feel free to contact

Zanthia via Facebook or Email
@
Wings of a Butterfly: The Poetic Justice of a
Domestic Abuse Survivor:
https://www.facebook.com/thewingsofabutterf
lyadvsurvivor?ref=hl

Zeveln Kesso: www.facebook.com/Onezant

By Email: zanthiak@gmail.com or
wingsofabutterflydvsurvivor@gmail.com

References

The Holy Bible. (2009) The New International Version. Grand Rapids, MI: Zondervan

Abbott, D., Lessons from the butterfly. Positive Butterfly. n.d. Retrieved from www.PositiveButterfly.com

Al-Modallal, H., Peden, A., & Anderson, D. (2008). Impact of physical abuse on adulthood depressive symptoms among women. Issues in Mental Health Nursing. *29(3), 299-314.*

Shahzadi, N., Qureshi, M., & Islam, M. (2012). Effect of domestic violence on women psychology in Pakistan. Language in India. *12(10), 293-311.*

(2014). Domestic violence against women: Recognize patterns, seek help. Mayo Clinic.

Clinton, T., Langberg, D. (2011). The quick-reference guide to counseling women.

Statistics. National Coalition of Domestic Violence. n.d.

Create a domestic violence safety plan. Safe Horizon. n.d.

Olsteen, J. (2015). A prayer for the day. Joel Olsteen Ministries.